3/12

D0007685

Elephants

Kate Davies

Illustrated by Rocío Martínez

Reading consultant: Alison Kelly
Roehampton University

The sun is rising.

A group of elephants stands
on a hot, grassy plain.

They have come to meet the
new baby of the family.

The newborn elephant blinks
in the sun.

Her legs are wobbly and
weak. At first she falls down.
But she tries again...

and again...

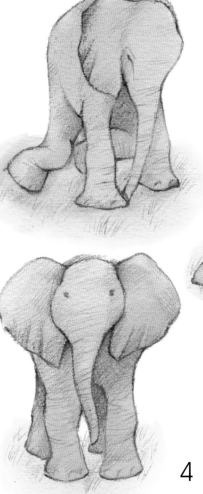

and soon she
can stand up.

4

Now she's very hungry.

So she drinks her
mother's milk.

She's a baby
African elephant.

Africa

Not all elephants
live in Africa.

Asia

China

India

Indian Ocean

Some come
from Asia.

African elephants are bigger
than Asian elephants.

Ear

Tusk

They have bigger ears
and longer tusks.

8

Tusks are really long,
pointy teeth.

Female Asian elephants
don't have tusks at all.

Every elephant has a tail,
to flick away flies,

four legs,

two small, black eyes

and a long,
bendy trunk.

11

An elephant's trunk is
like a really long nose.

But it's much more useful
than an ordinary nose.

12

The baby elephant
is learning to use
her trunk.

Her mother shows her all
the things she can do.

She picks leaves off the trees
and puts them in her mouth.

She sucks
up water in
her trunk.

And she squirts that
into her mouth, too.

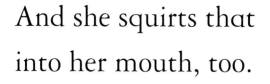

Elephants like to live in
hot places.

But they can live
almost anywhere.

They need water to drink,
and trees to shade them
from the sun.

Some Asian elephants live
in hot, wet rainforests.

Others live high up, near
tall mountains.

These Asian elephants live in a dry, dusty forest.

Every summer, the rain comes.

It falls for weeks.

The land gets flooded.

But the elephants
don't mind.

They like to swim.

Sometimes, baby elephants
hold on to their mothers' tails
in the water.

This keeps them safe as they
splash around.

25

In Africa, the elephants can't go swimming. It hasn't rained for months.

The trees and bushes are turning brown.

The water is drying up, too.

There's no food for the
elephants to eat.

27

So, the elephants go on a long journey to find food and water.

They travel in groups called herds.

They walk for hours
and hours.

At last, the elephants find a
pool of water.

The baby elephants play.

The adults drink...

and drink...

until they're full.

31

A lion is watching the elephant babies.

He spots one baby elephant,
standing alone...

But her mother hears the lion.
She flaps her ears,

lifts her trunk, and...

trumpets!

The lion slinks away.

The scared baby elephant
hides under her mother.

Female elephants live in
herds, with their babies.

Male elephants
live alone, or with
other males.

Sometimes male elephants fight. They want the females to notice them.

A female elephant chooses a male to be her partner.

They move away from the group together, for a while.

39

Soon, a baby elephant is growing inside the female.

It grows for nearly two years. At last, it is ready to be born.

The mother elephant slips
away from the herd.

Another female elephant
goes with her, to help.

The baby elephant is born
in the night.

The sun rises, and he blinks
his eyes.

The other elephants
gather around...

44

...to meet the new
baby of the family.

Elephant facts

- Elephants are the largest land animals in the world, and usually live between 50-70 years.

- There are about ten times as many African elephants as Asian elephants in the world.

- Elephants use their tusks to dig for food and fight. Just as humans are left- or right-handed, elephants are left- or right-tusked.

Index

African elephants, 6, 8

Asian elephants, 7-9

feeding, 5, 14-15

finding a partner, 38-40

herds, 28, 36-37

trunks, 11-15, 34

tusks, 8-9

Usborne Quicklinks

You can find out more about elephants by going to the Usborne Quicklinks Website at **www.usborne-quicklinks.com** and typing in the keywords "first reading elephants". Then click on the link for the website you want to visit. Please ask an adult before using the internet.

47

Internet Guidelines
The recommended websites are regularly reviewed and
updated but, please note, Usborne Publishing is not
responsible for the content of any website other than its
own. We recommend that young children are supervised
while on the internet.

Consultants: Zoological Society of London
Designed by Louise Flutter
Digital manipulation by Nick Wakeford
Series editor: Lesley Sims
Series designer: Russell Punter

First published in 2009 by Usborne Publishing Ltd.,
Usborne House, 83-85 Saffron Hill, London EC1N 8RT, England.
www.usborne.com Copyright © 2009 Usborne Publishing Ltd.

48

USBORNE FIRST READING
Level Four

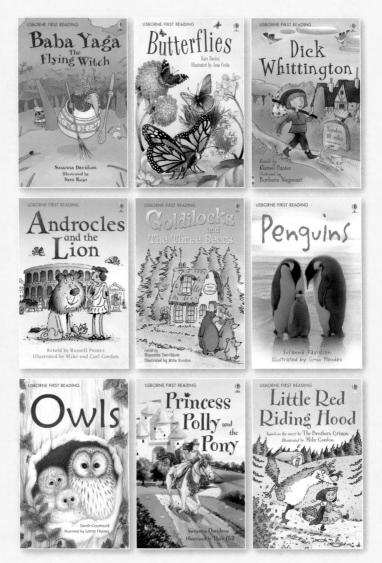